A Minor Poet and Other Verse

Amy Levy

A Minor Poet And other Verse

by

Amy Levy

Cameo Series T. Fisher Unwin

Paternoster Sq.

London E.C.

MDCCCXCI Second Edition

Note

This volume is a reprint of that issued in 1884, with the addition of a sonnet and a translation, from a volume published in Cambridge in 1881, and now out of print.

CONTENTS

- To a Dead Poet
- A Minor Poet
- Xantippe
- Medea
- Sinfonia Eroica
- To Sylvia
- A Greek Girl
- Magdalen
- Christopher Found
- A Dirge
- The Sick Man and the Nightingale
- To Death
- A June-Tide Echo
- To Lallie
- In a Minor Key
- A Farewell
- A Cross-Road Epitaph
- Epitaph
- Sonnet
- Translated from Geibel

A Minor Poet and Other Verse

To a Dead Poet.

I KNEW not if to laugh or weep ;
   They sat and talked of you—
"'Twas here he sat; 'twas this he said !
   'Twas that he used to do.

"Here is the book wherein he read,
   The room wherein he dwelt ;
And he" (they said) "was such a man,
   Such things he thought and felt."

I sat and sat, I did not stir ;
   They talked and talked away.
I was as mute as any stone,
   I had no word to say.

They talked and talked ; like to a stone
   My heart grew in my breast—
I, who had never seen your face
   Perhaps I knew you best.

A Minor Poet and Other Verse

A Minor Poet.

"What should such fellows as I do,
  Crawling between earth and heaven?"

Here is the phial ; here I turn the key
Sharp in the lock. Click !—there's no doubt it turned.
This is the third time ; there is luck in threes—
Queen Luck, that rules the world, befriend me now
And freely I'll forgive you many wrongs !
Just as the draught began to work, first time,
Tom Leigh, my friend (as friends go in the world),
Burst in, and drew the phial from my hand,
(Ah, Tom ! ah, Tom ! that was a sorry turn !)
And lectured me a lecture, all compact
Of neatest, newest phrases, freshly culled
From works of newest culture : "common good ;"
"The world's great harmonies ;""must be content
With knowing God works all things for the best,
And Nature never stumbles." Then again,
"The common good," and still, "the common, good ;"

And what a small thing was our joy or grief
When weigh'd with that of thousands. Gentle Tom,
But you might wag your philosophic tongue
From morn till eve, and still the thing's the same :
I am myself, as each man is himself—
Feels his own pain, joys his own joy, and loves
With his own love, no other's. Friend, the world
Is but one man ; one man is but the world.
And I am I, and you are Tom, that bleeds
When needles prick your flesh (mark, yours, not mine).
I must confess it; I can feel the pulse
A-beating at my heart, yet never knew
The throb of cosmic pulses. I lament
The death of youth's ideal in my heart ;
And, to be honest, never yet rejoiced
In the world's progress—scarce, indeed, discerned ;
(For still it seems that God's a Sisyphus
With the world for stone).
            You shake your head. I'm base,
Ignoble? Who is noble—you or I ?

I was not once thus ? Ah, my friend, we are
As the Fates make us.
                This time is the third ;
The second time the flask fell from my hand,

Its drowsy juices spilt upon the board ;
And there my face fell flat, and all the life
Crept from my limbs, and hand and foot were bound
With mighty chains, subtle, intangible ;
While still the mind held to its wonted use,
Or rather grew intense and keen with dread,
An awful dread—I thought I was in Hell.
In Hell, in Hell ! Was ever Hell conceived
By mortal brain, by brain Divine devised,
Darker, more fraught with torment, than the world
For such as I ? A creature maimed and marr'd
From very birth. A blot, a blur, a note
All out of tune in this world's instrument.
A base thing, yet not knowing to fulfil
Base functions. A high thing, yet all unmeet
For work that's high. A dweller on the earth,
Yet not content to dig with other men
Because of certain sudden sights and sounds
(Bars of broke music ; furtive, fleeting glimpse
Of angel faces 'thwart the grating seen)
Perceived in Heaven. Yet when I approach
To catch the sound's completeness, to absorb
The faces' full perfection, Heaven's gate,
Which then had stood ajar, sudden falls to,

And I, a-shiver in the dark and cold,
Scarce hear afar the mocking tones of men :
"He would not dig, forsooth ; but he must strive
For higher fruits than what our tillage yields ;
Behold what comes, my brothers, of vain pride !"
Why play with figures ? trifle prettily
With this my grief which very simply's said,
"There is no place for me in all the world" ?
The world's a rock, and I will beat no more
A breast of flesh and blood against a rock. . . .
A stride across the planks for old time's sake.
Ah, bare, small room that I have sorrowed in ;
Ay, and on sunny days, haply, rejoiced ;

We know some things together, you and I !
Hold there, you rangèd row of books ! In vain
You beckon from your shelf. You've stood my friends
Where all things else were foes ; yet now I'll turn
My back upon you, even as the world
Turns it on me. And yet—farewell, farewell !
You, lofty Shakespere, with the tattered leaves
And fathomless great heart, your binding's bruised
Yet did I love you less ? Goethe, farewell ;
Farewell, triumphant smile and tragic eyes,
And pitiless world-wisdom !

       For all men
These two. And 'tis farewell with you, my friends,
More dear because more near : Theokritus ;
Heine that stings and smiles ; Prometheus' bard ;
(I've grown too coarse for Shelley latterly :)
And one wild singer of to-day, whose song
Is all aflame with passionate bard's blood
Lash'd into foam by pain and the world's wrong.
At least, he has a voice to cry his pain ;
For him, no silent writhing in the dark,
No muttering of mute lips, no straining out
Of a weak throat a-choke with pent-up sound,
A-throb with pent-up passion. . . .
       Ah, my sun !
That's you, then, at the window, looking in
To beam farewell on one who's loved you long
And very truly. Up, you creaking thing,
You squinting, cobwebbed casement !
       So, at last,
I can drink in the sunlight. How it falls.
Across that endless sea of London roofs,
Weaving such golden wonders on the grey,
That almost, for the moment, we forget
The world of woe beneath them.
       Underneath,
For all the sunset glory, Pain is king.

Yet, the sun's there, and very sweet withal ;
And I'll not grumble that it's only sun,
But open wide my lips—thus—drink it in ;
Turn up my face to the sweet evening sky

(What royal wealth of scarlet on the blue
So tender toned, you'd almost think it green)
And stretch my hands out—so—to grasp it tight.
Ha, ha ! 'tis sweet awhile to cheat the Fates,
And be as happy as another man.
The sun works in my veins like wine, like wine !
'Tis a fair world : if dark, indeed, with woe,
Yet having hope and hint of such a joy,
That a man, winning, well might turn aside,
Careless of Heaven . . . .
                O enough ; I turn
From the sun's light, or haply I shall hope.
I have hoped enough ; I would not hope again :
'Tis hope that is most cruel.
                Tom, my friend,
You very sorry philosophic fool ;
'Tis you, I think, that bid me be resign'd,
Trust, and be thankful.
                Out on you ! Resign'd ?
I'm not resign'd, not patient, not school'd in
To take my starveling's portion and pretend
I'm grateful for it. I want all, all, all ;

I've appetite for all. I want the best :
Love, beauty, sunlight, nameless joy of life.
There's too much patience in the world, I think.
We have grown base with crooking of the knee.
Mankind—say—God has bidden to a feast ;
The board is spread, and groans with cates and drinks ;
In troop the guests ; each man with appetite
Keen-whetted with expectance.
                In they troop,
Struggle for seats, jostle and push and seize.
What's this ? what's this? There are not seats for all !
Some men must stand without the gates ; and some
Must linger by the table, ill-supplied
With broken meats. One man gets meat for two,
The while another hungers. If I stand
Without the portals, seeing others eat
Where I had thought to satiate the pangs
Of mine own hunger ; shall I then come forth
When all is done, and drink my Lord's good health
In my Lord's water ? Shall I not rather turn

And curse him, curse him for a niggard host ?
O, I have hungered, hungered, through the years,
Till appetite grows craving, then disease ;

I am starved, wither'd, shrivelled.
            Peace, O peace !
This rage is idle ; what avails to curse
The nameless forces, the vast silences
That work in all things.
            This time is the third,
I wrought before in heat, stung mad with pain,
Blind, scarcely understanding ; now I know
What thing I do.
            There was a woman once ;
Deep eyes she had, white hands, a subtle smile,
Soft speaking tones : she did not break my heart,
Yet haply had her heart been otherwise
Mine had not now been broken. Yet, who knows ?
My life was jarring discord from the first :
Tho' here and there brief hints of melody,
Of melody unutterable, clove the air.
From this bleak world, into the heart of night,
The dim, deep bosom of the universe,
I cast myself. I only crave for rest ;
Too heavy is the load. I fling it down.

EPILOGUE.

We knocked and knocked; at last, burst in the door,
And found him as you know — the outstretched arms

Propping the hidden face. The sun had set,
And all the place was dim with lurking shade.
There was no written word to say farewell,
Or make more clear the deed.
            I search'd and search'd ;
The room held little : just a row of books
Much scrawl'd and noted ; sketches on the wall,
Done rough in charcoal ; the old instrument
(A violin, no Stradivarius)
He played so ill on ; in the table drawer
Large schemes of undone work. Poems half-writ ;
Wild drafts of symphonies ; big plans of fugues ;

Some scraps of writing in a woman's hand :
No more—the scattered pages of a tale,
A sorry tale that no man cared to read.
Alas, my friend, I lov'd him well, tho' he
Held me a cold and stagnant-blooded fool,
Because I am content to watch, and wait
With a calm mind the issue of all things.
Certain it is my blood's no turbid stream ;
Yet, for all that, haply I understood
More than he ever deem'd ; nor held so light
The poet in him. Nay, I sometimes doubt
If they have not, indeed, the better part—
These poets, who get drunk with sun, and weep
Because the night or a woman's face is fair.

Meantime there is much talk about my friend.
The women say, of course, he died for love ;
The men, for lack of gold, or cavilling
Of carping critics. I, Tom Leigh, his friend
I have no word at all to say of this.
Nay, I had deem'd him more philosopher ;
For did he think by this one paltry deed
To cut the knot of circumstance, and snap
The chain which binds all being ?

Xantippe.

(A FRAGMENT.)

"Xantippe" has appeared in the University Magazine, and in a collection of Verse published at Cambridge.

WHAT, have I waked again ? I never thought
To see the rosy dawn, or ev'n this grey,
Dull, solemn stillness, ere the dawn has come.
The lamp burns low ; low burns the lamp of life :
The still morn stays expectant, and my soul,
All weighted with a passive wonderment,
Waiteth and watcheth, waiteth for the dawn.
Come hither, maids ; too soundly have ye slept
That should have watched me ; nay, I would not chide—
Oft have I chidden, yet I would not chide
In this last hour ;—now all should be at peace.
I have been dreaming in a troubled sleep
Of weary days I thought not to recall ;
Of stormy days, whose storms are hushed long since ;

Of gladsome days, of sunny days ; alas
In dreaming, all their sunshine seem'd so sad,
As though the current of the dark To-Be
Had flow'd, prophetic, through the happy hours.
And yet, full well, I know it was not thus ;
I mind me sweetly of the summer days,
When, leaning from the lattice, I have caught
The fair, far glimpses of a shining sea ;
And, nearer, of tall ships which thronged the bay,
And stood out blackly from a tender sky
All flecked with sulphur, azure, and bright gold ;
And in the still, clear air have heard the hum
Of distant voices ; and methinks there rose
No darker fount to mar or stain the joy
Which sprang ecstatic in my maiden breast
Than just those vague desires, those hopes and fears,
Those eager longings, strong, though undefined,
Whose very sadness makes them seem so sweet.
What cared I for the merry mockeries
Of other maidens sitting at the loom ?

Or for sharp voices, bidding me return
To maiden labour ? Were we not apart—
I and my high thoughts, and my golden dreams,
My soul which yearned for knowledge, for a tongue
That should proclaim the stately mysteries

Of this fair world, and of the holy gods ?
Then followed days of sadness, as I grew
To learn my woman-mind had gone astray,
And I was sinning in those very thoughts—
For maidens, mark, such are not woman's thoughts—
(And yet, 'tis strange, the gods who fashion us
Have given us such promptings). . . .
         Fled the years,
Till seventeen had found me tall and strong,
And fairer, runs it, than Athenian maids
Are wont to seem ; I had not learnt it well—
My lesson of dumb patience—and I stood
At Life's great threshold with a beating heart,
And soul resolved to conquer and attain. . . .
Once, walking 'thwart the crowded market-place,
With other maidens, bearing in the twigs
White doves for Aphrodite's sacrifice,
I saw him, all ungainly and uncouth,
Yet many gathered round to hear his words,
Tall youths and stranger-maidens—Sokrates—
I saw his face and marked it, half with awe,
Half with a quick repulsion at the shape. . . .
The richest gem lies hidden furthest down,
And is the dearer for the weary search ;
We grasp the shining shells which strew the shore,

Yet swift we fling them from us ; but the gem
We keep for aye and cherish. So a soul,
Found after weary searching in the flesh
Which half repelled our senses, is more dear,
For that same seeking, than the sunny mind
Which lavish Nature marks with thousand hints
Upon a brow of beauty. We are prone
To overweigh such subtle hints, then deem,
In after disappointment, we are fooled. . . .
And when, at length, my father told me all,
That I should wed me with great Sokrates,

I, foolish, wept to see at once cast down
The maiden image of a future love,
Where perfect body matched the perfect soul.
But slowly, softly did I cease to weep ;
Slowly I 'gan to mark the magic flash
Leap to the eyes, to watch the sudden smile
Break round the mouth, and linger in the eyes ;
To listen for the voice's lightest tone —
Great voice, whose cunning modulations seemed
Like to the notes of some sweet instrument.
So did I reach and strain, until at last
I caught the soul athwart the grosser flesh.
Again of thee, sweet Hope, my spirit dreamed !
I, guided by his wisdom and his love,
Led by his words, and counselled by his care,

Should lift the shrouding veil from things which be,
And at the flowing fountain of his soul
Refresh my thirsting spirit. . . .
          And indeed,
In those long days which followed that strange day
When rites and song, and sacrifice and flow'rs,
Proclaimed that we were wedded, did I learn,
In sooth, a-many lessons ; bitter ones
Which sorrow taught me, and not love inspired,
Which deeper knowledge of my kind impressed
With dark insistence on reluctant brain ;—
But that great wisdom, deeper, which dispels
Narrowed conclusions of a half-grown mind,
And sees athwart the littleness of life
Nature's divineness and her harmony,
Was never poor Xantippe's. . . .
          I would pause
And would recall no more, no more of life,
Than just the incomplete, imperfect dream
Of early summers, with their light and shade,
Their blossom-hopes, whose fruit was never ripe ;
But something strong within me, some sad chord
Which loudly echoes to the later life,
Me to unfold the after-misery

Urges, with plaintive wailing in my heart.
Yet, maidens, mark ; I would not that ye thought

I blame my lord departed, for he meant
No evil, so I take it, to his wife.
'Twas only that the high philosopher,
Pregnant with noble theories and great thoughts,
Deigned not to stoop to touch so slight a thing
As the fine fabric of a woman's brain—
So subtle as a passionate woman's soul.
I think, if he had stooped a little, and cared,
I might have risen nearer to his height,
And not lain shattered, neither fit for use
As goodly household vessel, nor for that
Far finer thing which I had hoped to be. . . .
Death, holding high his retrospective lamp,
Shows me those first, far years of wedded life,
Ere I had learnt to grasp the barren shape
Of what the Fates had destined for my life
Then, as all youthful spirits are, was I
Wholly incredulous that Nature meant
So little, who had promised me so much.
At first I fought my fate with gentle words,
With high endeavours after greater things ;
Striving to win the soul of Sokrates,
Like some slight bird, who sings her burning love
To human master, till at length she finds

Her tender language wholly misconceived,
And that same hand whose kind caress she sought,
With fingers flippant flings the careless corn. . . .
I do remember how, one summer's eve,
He, seated in an arbour's leafy shade,
Had bade me bring fresh wine-skins. . . .
           As I stood
Ling'ring upon the threshold, half concealed
By tender foliage, and my spirit light
With draughts of sunny weather, did I mark
An instant the gay group before mine eyes.
Deepest in shade, and facing where I stood,
Sat Plato, with his calm face and low brows
Which met above the narrow Grecian eyes,
The pale, thin lips just parted to the smile,
Which dimpled that smooth olive of his cheek.
His head a little bent, sat Sokrates,
With one swart finger raised admonishing,

And on the air were borne his changing tones.
Low lounging at his feet, one fair arm thrown
Around his knee (the other, high in air
Brandish'd a brazen amphor, which yet rained
Bright drops of ruby on the golden locks
And temples with their fillets of the vine),
Lay Alkibiades the beautiful.
And thus, with solemn tone, spake Sokrates :

" This fair Aspasia, which our Perikles
Hath brought from realms afar, and set on high
In our Athenian city, hath a mind,
I doubt not, of a strength beyond her race ;
And makes employ of it, beyond the way
Of women nobly gifted : woman's frail—
Her body rarely stands the test of soul ;
She grows intoxicate with knowledge ; throws
The laws of custom, order, 'neath her feet,
Feasting at life's great banquet with wide throat."
Then sudden, stepping from my leafy screen,
Holding the swelling wine-skin o'er my head,
With breast that heaved, and eyes and cheeks aflame,
Lit by a fury and a thought, I spake :
" By all great powers around us ! can it be
That we poor women are empirical ?
That gods who fashioned us did strive to make
Beings too fine, too subtly delicate,
With sense that thrilled response to ev'ry touch
Of nature's, and their task is not complete ?
That they have sent their half-completed work
To bleed and quiver here upon the earth ?
To bleed and quiver, and to weep and weep,
To beat its soul against the marble walls
Of men's cold hearts, and then at last to sin !"

I ceased, the first hot passion stayed and stemmed
And frighted by the silence : I could see,
Framed by the arbour foliage, which the sun
In setting softly gilded with rich gold,
Those upturned faces, and those placid limbs ;
Saw Plato's narrow eyes and niggard mouth,
Which half did smile and half did criticise,
One hand held up, the shapely fingers framed

To gesture of entreaty—" Hush, I pray,
Do not disturb her ; let us hear the rest ;
Follow her mood, for here's another phase
Of your black-browed Xantippe. . . ."
         Then I saw
Young Alkibiades, with laughing lips
And half-shut eyes, contemptuous shrugging up
Soft, snowy shoulders, till he brought the gold
Of flowing ringlets round about his breasts.
But Sokrates, all slow and solemnly,
Raised, calm, his face to mine, and sudden spake :
" I thank thee for the wisdom which thy lips
Have thus let fall among us : prythee tell
From what high source, from what philosophies
Didst cull the sapient notion of thy words ?"
Then stood I straight and silent for a breath,
Dumb, crushed with all that weight of cold contempt ;

But swiftly in my bosom there uprose
A sudden flame, a merciful fury sent
To save me ; with both angry hands I flung
The skin upon the marble, where it lay
Spouting red rills and fountains on the white ;
Then, all unheeding faces, voices, eyes,
I fled across the threshold, hair unbound—
White garment stained to redness—beating heart
Flooded with all the flowing tide of hopes
Which once had gushed out golden, now sent back
Swift to their sources, never more to rise. . . .
I think I could have borne the weary life,
The narrow life within the narrow walls,
If he had loved me ; but he kept his love
For this Athenian city and her sons ;
And, haply, for some stranger-woman, bold
With freedom, thought, and glib philosophy. . . .
Ah me ! the long, long weeping through the nights,
The weary watching for the pale-eyed dawn
Which only brought fresh grieving : then I grew
Fiercer, and cursed from out my inmost heart
The Fates which marked me an Athenian maid.
Then faded that vain fury ; hope died out ;
A huge despair was stealing on my soul,

A sort of fierce acceptance of my fate,—
He wished a household vessel—well 'twas good,
For he should have it ! He should have no more
The yearning treasure of a woman's love,
But just the baser treasure which he sought.
I called my maidens, ordered out the loom,
And spun unceasing from the morn till eve ;
Watching all keenly over warp and woof,
Weighing the white wool with a jealous hand.
I spun until, methinks, I spun away
The soul from out my body, the high thoughts
From out my spirit ; till at last I grew
As ye have known me,—eye exact to mark
The texture of the spinning ; ear all keen
For aimless talking when the moon is up,
And ye should be a-sleeping ; tongue to cut
With quick incision, 'thwart the merry words
Of idle maidens. . . .
        Only yesterday
My hands did cease from spinning ; I have wrought
My dreary duties, patient till the last.
The gods reward me ! Nay, I will not tell
The after years of sorrow ; wretched strife
With grimmest foes—sad Want and Poverty ;—
Nor yet the time of horror, when they bore

My husband from the threshold ; nay, nor when
The subtle weed had wrought its deadly work.
Alas ! alas ! I was not there to soothe
The last great moment ; never any thought
Of her that loved him—save at least the charge,
All earthly, that her body should not starve. . . .
You weep, you weep ; I would not that ye wept ;
Such tears are idle ; with the young, such grief
Soon grows to gratulation, as, "her love
Was withered by misfortune ; mine shall grow
All nurtured by the loving," or, "her life
Was wrecked and shattered—mine shall smoothly sail."
Enough, enough. In vain, in vain, in vain !
The gods forgive me ! Sorely have I sinned
In all my life. A fairer fate befall
You all that stand there. . . .
        Ha ! the dawn has come ;

I see a rosy glimmer—nay ! it grows dark ;
Why stand ye so in silence ? throw it wide,
The casement, quick ; why tarry ?—give me air—
O fling it wide, I say, and give me light !

Medea.

(A Fragment in Drama Form, After Euripides.)

panton d'os est' empsuxa kai
gnomen exei gunaikes esmen
athliotaton phuton.

Persons.
- Medea.
- Jason.

Citizens of Corinth.
o Ægeus.
o Nikias.

Scene : Before Medea's House.

[Enter Medea.]

Medea.

TO-DAY, to-day, I know not why it is,
I do bethink me of my Colchian home.
To-day, that I am lone and weary and sad,
I fain would call back days of pride and hope ;
Of pride in strength, when strength was all unprov'd,
Of hope too high, too sweet, to be confined
In limits of conception.

    I am sad
Here in this gracious city, whose white walls
Gleam snow-like in the sunlight ; whose fair shrines
Are filled with wondrous images of gods ;
Upon whose harbour's bosom ride tall ships,
Black-masted, fraught with fragrant merchandise ;
Whose straight-limbed people, in fair stuffs arrayed,
Do throng from morn till eve the sunny streets.
For what avail fair shrines and images ?
What, cunning workmanship and purple robes ?
Light of sweet sunlight, play and spray of waves ?
When all around the air is charged and chill,

And all the place is drear and dark with hate ?
Alas, alas, this people loves me not !
This strong, fair people, marble-cold and smooth
As modelled marble. I, an alien here,
That well can speak the language of their lips,
The language of their souls may never learn.
And in their hands, I, that did know myself
Ere now, a creature in whose veins ran blood
Redder, more rapid, than flows round most hearts,
Do seem a creature reft of life and soul.
If they would only teach the subtle trick

By which their hearts are melted into love,
I'd strive to learn it. I am very meek.
They think me proud, but I am very meek,
Ready to do their bidding. Hear me, friends !
Friends, I am very hungry, give me love !
'Tis all I ask ! is it so hard to give ?
You stand and front me with your hostile eyes ;
You only give me hatred ?
    Yet I know
Ye are not all unloving. Oft I see
The men and women walking in the ways,
Hand within hand, and tender-bated breath,
On summer evenings when the sky is fair.
O men and women, are ye then so hard ?
Will ye not give a little of your love
To me that am so hungry ?

  Enter Ægeus and Nikias, on the opposite side. Medea steps
  back on the threshold and pauses.]

    Ha, that word !
'Tis Jason's name they bandy to and fro.
I know not why, whene'er his name is spoke,
Once name of joy and ever name of love,
I wax white and do tremble ; sudden seized
With shadowy apprehension. May't forbode
No evil unto him I hold so dear ;

And ever dearer with the waxing years :—
For this indeed is woman's chiefest curse,
That still her constant heart clings to its love

Through all time and all chances ; while the man
Is caught with newness ; coldly calculates,
And measures pain and pleasure, loss and gain ;
And ever grows to look with the world's eye
Upon a woman, tho' his, body and soul.   [She goes within.]

   [The two citizens come forward.]

   Nikias.
I, in this thing, do hold our Jason wise ;
Kreon is mighty ; Glaukê very fair.

   Ægeus.
An 'twere for that—the Colchian's fair enough.

   Nikias.
I like not your swart skins and purple hair ;
Your black, fierce eyes where the brows meet across.
By all the gods ! when yonder Colchian
Fixes me with her strange and sudden gaze,
Each hair upon my body stands erect !
Zeus, 'tis a very tiger, and as mute !

   Ægeus.
'Tis certain that the woman's something strange.

   Nikias.
Gods, spare me your strange women, so say I.
Give me gold hair, lithe limbs and gracious smiles,
And spare the strangeness.

   Ægeus.
         I do marvel much
How she will bear the tidings.

   Nikias.
         Lo, behold !
Here comes our Jason striding 'thwart the streets.
Gods ! what a gracious presence !

   Ægeus.
         I perceive
The Colchian on the threshold. By her looks,

Our idle talk has reached her listening ears.

[Enter Jason. Medea reappears on the threshold.]

Nikias.
Let's draw aside and mark them ; lo, they meet.

[The two citizens withdraw, unperceived, to a further corner of the stage.]

Medea.
'Tis false, 'tis false. O Jason, they speak false !

Jason.
Your looks are wild, Medea ; you bring shame
Upon this house, that stand with hair unbound
Beyond the threshold. Get you in the house.

Medea.
But not till you have answered me this thing.

Jason.
What is this thing that you would know of me ?

Medea.
O I have heard strange rumours—horrible !

Jason.
Oft lies the horror of a tale in the ear
Of him that hears it. What is 't you have heard ?

Medea.
Almost, for fear, I dare not give it tongue.
But tell me this ? Love, you have not forgot
The long years passed in this Corinthian home ?
The great love I have borne you through the years ?
Nor that far time when, in your mighty craft,
You came, a stranger, to the Colchian shore ?
O strong you were ; but not of such a strength
To have escaped the doom of horrid death,
Had not I, counting neither loss nor gain,
Shown you the way to triumph and renown.

Jason.
And better had I then, a thousand times,
Have fought with my good sword and fall'n or stood
As the high Fates directed ; than been caught
In the close meshes of the magic web
Wrought by your hand, dark-thoughted sorceress.

Nikias.
Did you mark that ? Jason speaks low and smooth ;
Yet there is that within his level tones,

And in the icy drooping of his lids
(More than his words, tho' they are harsh enough),
Tells me he hates her.

Ægeus.
    Hush ! Medea speaks.

Medea.
O gods, gods ; ye have cursed me in this gift !
Is it for this, for this that I have striven ?
Have wrestled in the darkness ? wept my tears ?
Have fought with sweet desires and hopes and thoughts ?
Have watched when men were sleeping ? for long days
Have shunned the sunlight and the breaths of Heaven ?
Is it for this, for this that I have prayed
Long prayers, poured out with blood and cries and tears ?
Lo, I who strove for strength have grown more weak
Than is the weakest. I have poured the sap
Of all my being, my life's very life,
Before a thankless godhead ; and am grown

No woman, but a monster. What avail
Charms, spells and potions, all my hard-won arts,
My mystic workings, seeing they cannot win
One little common spark of human love ?
O gods, gods, ye have cursed me in this gift !
More should ye have withheld or more have giv'n ;
Have fashioned me more weak or else more strong.
Behold me now, your work, a thing of fear—
From natural human fellowship cut off,
And yet a woman—sick and sore with pain ;
Hungry for love and music of men's praise,

But walled about as with a mighty wall,
Far from men's reach and sight, alone, alone.

   Nikias.
Behold her, how she waves about her arms
And casts her eyes to Heaven.

   Ægeus.
          Ay, 'tis strange—
Not as our women do, yet scarce unmeet.

   Nikias.
Unmeet, unmeet ? But Jason holds it so !

Mark you his white cheeks and his knitted brows,
What wrath and hate and scorn upon his face !

   Jason.
Hear me, Medea, if you still can hear
That seem so strangely lifted from yourself :
But I, that know you long, do know you well,
A thing of moods and passions ; so I bear
Once more with your wild words and savage gests,
Ay, and for all your fury speak you fair.
You say you love me. Can I deem it so,
When what does most advantage me and mine
You shrink to hear of ? For I make no doubt,
Fleet-footed rumour did anticipate
The tidings I was hastening to bear,
When you, wide-eyed, unveiled, unfilleted,
Rushed out upon me.
          Know then this once more :
That I have sworn to take as wedded wife
Glaukê, the daughter of our mighty king,
In this, in nowise hurting you and yours.
For you all fair provisions I have made,
So but you get beyond the city walls
Before the night comes on. Our little ones—
They too shall journey with you. I have said.

And had I found you in a mood more mild,
Less swayed by savage passion, I had told
How this thing, which mayhap seems a thing hard,

Is but a blessing, wrapped and cloaked about
In harsh disguisements. For tho' Kreon rule
To-day within the city ; Kreon dead,
Who else shall rule there saving I alone,
The king's son loved of him and other men ?
And in those days Medea's sons and mine
Shall stand at my right hand, grown great in power.
Medea, too, if she do but control
Her fiery spirit, may yet reign a queen
Above this land of Corinth. I have said.

   Nikias.
Well said.

   Ægeus.
        But none the better that 'twas false.

   Nikias.
I'd sooner speak, for my part, fair than true.
Mark Jason there ; how firm his lithe, straight limbs ;
How high his gold-curled head, crisped like a girl's.

And yet for all his curled locks and smooth tones
Jason is very strong. I never knew
A man of such a strange and subtle strength.

   Ægeus.
The Colchian speaks no word ; and her swart hands,
Which waved, a moment since, and beat the air
In mad entreaty, are together clasped
Before her white robe in an iron clasp.
And her wild eyes, which erst did seek the heav'ns,
And now her lord and now again the earth,
Are set on space and move not. The tall shape
Stands there erect and still. This calm, I think,
Is filled with strangest portent.

   Nikias.
       O ye gods,
She is a pregnant horror as she stands.

   Ægeus.
She speaks ; her voice sounds as a sound far off.

   Medea.
As you have said, O Jason, let it be.

I for my part am nothing loth to break
A compact never in fair justice framed,
Seeing how much one gave and one how much.
For you, you thought : This maid has served me well,
And yet may serve me. When I touch her palm
The blood is set a-tingle in my veins ;
For these things I will make her body mine.
And I, I stood before you, clean and straight,
A woman some deemed fair and all deemed wise ;
A woman, yet no simple thing nor slight,
By nature fashioned in no niggard mould ;
And looked into your eyes with eyes that spake :
Lo, utterly, for ever, I am yours.
And since that you, this gift I lavish laid
Low at your feet, have lightly held and spurned —
I in my two arms, thus, shall gather it up
So that your feet may not encounter it
Which is not worthy for your feet to tread !
Yet pause a moment, Jason. Haply now
In some such wise as this your thoughts run on :
I loved this woman for a little space ;
Alas, poor soul, she loved me but too well —
It is the way with women ! Some, I think,
Did deem her fierce ; gods ! she was meek enough,

Content with what I gave ; when I gave not
Nothing importunate.
        Ah, Jason, pause.
You never knew Medea. You forget,
Because so long she bends the knee to you,
She was not born to serfdom.
        I have knelt
Too long before you. I have stood too long
Suppliant before this people. You forget
A redder stream flows in my Colchian veins
Than the slow flood which courses round your hearts,
O cold Corinthians, with whom I long have dwelt
And never ere this day have known myself.
Nor have ye known me. Now behold me free,
Ungyved by any chains of this man wrought ;

Nothing desiring at your hands nor his.
Free, freer than the air or wingèd birds ;
Strong, stronger than the blast of wintry storms ;
And lifted up into an awful realm
Where is nor love, nor pity, nor remorse,
Nor dread, but only purpose.
            There shall be
A horror and a horror in this land ;
Woe upon woe, red blood and biting flame ;

Most horrid death and anguish worse than death ;
Deeds that shall make the shores of Hades sound
With murmured terror ; with an awful dread
Shall move the generations yet unborn ;
A horror and a horror in the land.

  Jason.
Shrew, triple-linked with Hell, get you within.
Shame not my house ! 'Tis your own harm you work.

    [Medea goes within. Jason moves off slowly. Ægeus and Nikias go off conferring in whispers.]

Scene II

    [Time—After an interval ; the evening of the same day. Scene—A street. A crowd of people running to and fro.]

  Nikias.
O horror, horror, have ye heard the tale ?

  Ægeus.
Alas, a bloody rumour reached mine ears
Of awful purport : that the king lies dead—

  Nikias.
And by his side, his daughter ; both caught up
In sudden toils of torment. With his grief
Jason is all distraught ; behold her deed,
The swift and subtle tigress !

Ægeus.
        Woe ! Alas !
Woe for the state, woe for our Kreon slain,
For hapless Glaukê, for our Jason, woe !
But three times woe for her that did the deed—
Her womanhood sham'd ; her children basely wrong'd.

Nikias.
Hold back our pity till the tale be told,
For never was there horror like to this.
Ere now in Corinth, haply, you have heard
How she did use for her crime's instruments
The tender boys sprung from great Jason's loins ;
Bidding them bear the garments wrought in Hell
As bridal gifts to grace the marriage morn
Of gold-hair'd Glaukê. Serpent ! Sorceress !

Ægeus.
Alas, consider ; so the tigress springs

When that her cubs are menaced. 'Twas her love
That wrought the deed—evil, yet wrought for love.

Nikias.
Spare me such love. I never yet could deem,
Ev'n ere the horror, that Medea held
The love of human mothers in her breast.
For I have seen her, when her children played
Their innocent, aimless sports about her knees,
Or held her gown across the market-place,
Move all unheeding with her swart brows knit
And fierce eyes fixed ; not, as is mothers' wont,
Eager to note the winning infant ways,
A-strain to catch the babbling treble tones
Of soft lips clamouring for a kiss or smile.
And once I marked her ('twas a summer's morn)
Turn suddenly and, stooping, catch and strain
One tender infant to her breast. She held
Her lips to his and looked into his eyes,
Not gladly, as a mother with her child,
But stirred by some strange passion ; then the boy
Cried out with terror, and Medea wept.

Ægeus.
Your tale is strange.

  Nikias.
        Stranger is yet to come.
How that the Colchian did send forth her sons,
Innocent doers of most deadly deed,
Has reached your knowledge. When the deed was done,
And the dead king lay stretched upon the floor
Clutching his daughter in a last embrace,
Arose great clamour in the palace halls ;
Wailing and cries of terror ; women's screams ;
A rush of flying feet from hall to hall ;
The clanging fall of brazen instruments
Upon the marble.
      The two tender boys,
Half apprehending what thing had befallen,
Fled forth unmarked, and all affrighted reached
The house of Jason, where Medea stood
Erect upon the threshold. From afar
Sounded and surged the fiercely frighted roar
Of the roused city, and, like waves of the sea,
Grew nearer ev'ry beating of the pulse.
Forth from the inmost chambers fled the slaves,
Made fleet with sudden fear ; the little ones

With arms outspread rushed to the Colchian,
And clung about her limbs and caught her robe,
Hiding their faces.
      And Medea stood
Calm as a carven image. As the sound
Of wrath and lamentation drew more near,
The pale lips seemed to smile. But when she saw
Her children clinging round her, she stretched forth
One strong, swart hand and put the twain away,
And gathered up the trailing of her robe.
I saw the deed, I, Nikias, with these eyes !
Then spake she (Zeus ! grant that I may not hear
Such tones once more from human lips !). She spake :
"I will not have ye, for I love ye not !"
Then all her face grew alien. Those around
Stood still, not knowing what she planned.
                Then she

Forth from her gathered garment swiftly drew
A thing that gleamed and glinted ; in the air
She held it poised an instant ; then—O gods !
How shall I speak it ?—on the marble floor
Was blood that streamed and spurted ; blood that flow'd
From two slain, innocent babes !

  Ægeus.
        O woful day !

  Nikias.
Then brake a cry from all about : a wail
Of lamentation. But above the sound
A fierce long shriek, that froze the blood i' the veins,
Rang out and rose, cleaving the topmost cloud.
  Ægeus.
O evil deed ! O essence of all evil
Stealing the shape of woman !

  Nikias.
       After that
All is confusion ; from all sides surged up
The people, cursing, weeping. 'Thwart the din
Each other moment the strained ear might catch
Medea's name, or Jason's, or the King's ;
And women wailed out "Glaukê" through their tears.
Then sudden came a pause ; the angry roar
Died down into a murmur ; and the throng
Grew still, and rolled aside like a clov'n sea.

And Jason strode between them till he reached
His own home's threshold where the twain lay dead,
Long gazed he on their faces ; then he turned
To the hush'd people ; turned to them and spake :
(His face was whiter than the dead's, his eyes
Like to a creature's that has looked on Hell)
"Where is the woman ?" Lo, and when they sought
Medea, no eye beheld her. And no man
Had looked upon her since that moment's space
When steel had flashed and blood foamed in the air.
Then Jason stood erect and spake again :
"Let no man seek this woman ; blood enough
Has stained our city. Let the furies rend

Her guilty soul ; nor we pollute our hands
With her accursèd body . . ."

  Ægeus.
                Cease, my friend ;
It is enough. You judged this thing aright ;
This woman was dark and evil in her soul ;
Black to her fiend-heart's root ; a festering plague
In our fair city's midst.

  Nikias.
                Spake I not true?
[Night ; outside the city. Medea leaning against a rock.]
Here let me rest ; beyond men's eyes, beyond
The city's hissing hate. Why am I here ?
Why have I fled from death ? There's sun on the earth,
And in the shades no sun ;—thus much I know ;
And sunlight's good.
              Wake I, or do I sleep ?
I'm weary, weary ; once I dream'd a dream
Of one that strove and wept and yearned for love
In a fair city. She was blind indeed.
They say the woman had a fiend at heart,
And afterwards—Hush, hush, I dream'd a dream.
How cold the air blows ; how the night grows dark,
Wrapping me round in blackness. Darker too
Grows the deep night within. I cannot see ;
I grope with weary hands ; my hands are sore
With fruitless striving. I have fought with the Fates
And I am vanquished utterly. The Fates
Yield not to strife; nay, nor to many prayers.

Their ways are dark.
           One climbs the tree and grasps
A handful of dead leaves ; another walks,
Heedless, beneath the branches, and the fruit
Falls mellow at his feet.
            This is the end :
I have dash'd my heart against a rock ; the blood
Is drain'd and flows no more ; and all my breast
Is emptied of its tears.
            Thus go I forth
Into the deep, dense heart of the night—alone.

Sinfonia Eroica.

(To Sylvia.)

MY Love, my Love, it was a day in June,
A mellow, drowsy, golden afternoon ;
And all the eager people thronging came
To that great hall, drawn by the magic name
Of one, a high magician, who can raise
The spirits of the past and future days,
And draw the dreams from out the secret breast,
Giving them life and shape.
   I, with the rest,
Sat there athirst, atremble for the sound ;
And as my aimless glances wandered round,
Far off, across the hush'd, expectant throng,
I saw your face that fac'd mine.
   Clear and strong
Rush'd forth the sound, a mighty mountain stream ;
Across the clust'ring heads mine eyes did seem
By subtle forces drawn, your eyes to meet.
Then you, the melody, the summer heat,
Mingled in all my blood and made it wine.
Straight I forgot the world's great woe and mine ;
My spirit's murky lead grew molten fire ;
Despair itself was rapture.
   Ever higher,
Stronger and clearer rose the mighty strain ;
Then sudden fell ; then all was still again,
And I sank back, quivering as one in pain.
Brief was the pause ; then, 'mid a hush profound,
Slow on the waiting air swell'd forth a sound
So wondrous sweet that each man held his breath ;
A measur'd, mystic melody of death.
Then back you lean'd your head, and I could note
The upward outline of your perfect throat ;
And ever, as the music smote the air,
Mine eyes from far held fast your body fair.
And in that wondrous moment seem'd to fade
My life's great woe, and grow an empty shade
Which had not been, nor was not.
   And I knew
Not which was sound, and which, O Love, was you.

To Sylvia.

"O LOVE, lean thou thy cheek to mine,
And let the tears together flow" —
Such was the song you sang to me
    Once, long ago.

Such was the song you sang ; and yet
(O be not wroth !) I scarcely knew
What sounds flow'd forth ; I only felt
    That you were you.

I scarcely knew your hair was gold,
Nor of the heavens' own blue your eyes.
Sylvia and song, divinely mixt,
    Made Paradise.

These things I scarcely knew ; to-day,
When love is lost and hope is fled,
The song you sang so long ago
    Rings in my head.

Clear comes each note and true ; to-day,
As in a picture I behold
Your tur'd-up chin, and small, sweet head
    Misty with gold.

I see how your dear eyes grew deep,
How your lithe body thrilled and swayed,
And how were whiter than the keys
    Your hands that played. . . .

Ah, sweetest ! cruel have you been,
And robbed my life of many things.
I will not chide ; ere this I knew
    That Love had wings.

You've robbed my life of many things—
Of love and hope, of fame and pow'r.
So be it, sweet. You cannot steal
    One golden hour.

A Greek Girl.

I MAY not weep, not weep, and he is dead.
A weary, weary weight of tears unshed
Through the long day in my sad heart I bear ;
The horrid sun with all unpitying glare
Shines down into the dreary weaving-room,
Where clangs the ceaseless clatter of the loom,
And ceaselessly deft maiden-fingers weave
The fine-wrought web ; and I from morn till eve
Work with the rest, and when folk speak to me
I smile hard smiles ; while still continually
The silly stream of maiden speech flows on :—
And now at length they talk of him that's gone,
Lightly lamenting that he died so soon—
Ah me ! ere yet his life's sun stood at noon.
Some praise his eyes, some deem his body fair,
And some mislike the colour of his hair !
Sweet life, sweet shape, sweet eyes, and sweetest hair,
What form, what hue, save Love's own, did ye wear ?
I may not weep, not weep, for very shame.

He loved me not. One summer's eve he came
To these our halls, my father's honoured guest,
And seeing me, saw not. If his lips had prest
My lips, but once, in love ; his eyes had sent
One love-glance into mine, I had been content,
And deemed it great joy for one little life ;
Nor envied other maids the crown of wife :
The long sure years, the merry children-band—
Alas, alas, I never touched his hand !
And now my love is dead that loved not me.
Thrice-blest, thrice-crowned, of gods thrice-lovèd she—
That other, fairer maid, who tombward brings
Her gold, shorn locks and piled-up offerings
Of fragrant fruits, rich wines, and spices rare,
And cakes with honey sweet, with saffron fair ;
And who, unchecked by any thought of shame,
May weep her tears, and call upon his name,
With burning bosom prest to the cold ground,
Knowing, indeed, that all her life is crown'd,
Thrice-crowned, thrice honoured, with that love of his ;—

No dearer crown on earth is there, I wis.
While yet the sweet life lived, more light to bear

Was my heart's hunger ; when the morn was fair,
And I with other maidens in a line
Passed singing through the city to the shrine,
Oft in the streets or crowded market-place
I caught swift glimpses of the dear-known face ;
Or marked a stalwart shoulder in the throng ;
Or heard stray speeches as we passed along,
In tones more dear to me than any song.
These, hoarded up with care, and kept apart,
Did serve as meat and drink my hungry heart.
And now for ever has my sweet love gone ;
And weary, empty days I must drag on,
Till all the days of all my life be sped,
By no thought cheered, by no hope comforted.
For if indeed we meet among the shades,
How shall he know me from the other maids ?—
Me, that had died to save his body pain !
Alas, alas, such idle thoughts are vain !
O cruel, cruel sunlight, get thee gone !
O dear, dim shades of eve, come swiftly on !
That when quick lips, keen eyes, are closed in sleep,
Through the long night till dawn I then may weep.

Magdalen.

ALL things I can endure, save one.
The bare, blank room where is no sun ;
The parcelled hours ; the pallet hard ;
The dreary faces here within ;
The outer women's cold regard ;
The Pastor's iterated "sin" ;—
These things could I endure, and count
No overstrain'd, unjust amount ;
No undue payment for such bliss—
Yea, all things bear, save only this :
That you, who knew what thing would be,
Have wrought this evil unto me.
It is so strange to think on still—
That you, that you should do me ill !
Not as one ignorant or blind,
But seeing clearly in your mind
How this must be which now has been,
Nothing aghast at what was seen.
Now that the tale is told and done,
It is so strange to think upon.

You were so tender with me, too !
One summer's night a cold blast blew,
Closer about my throat you drew
The half-slipt shawl of dusky blue.
And once my hand, on a summer's morn,
I stretched to pluck a rose ; a thorn
Struck through the flesh and made it bleed
(A little drop of blood indeed !)
Pale grew your cheek ; you stoopt and bound
Your handkerchief about the wound ;
Your voice came with a broken sound ;
With the deep breath your breast was riven ;
I wonder, did God laugh in Heaven ?
How strange, that you should work my woe !
How strange ! I wonder, do you know
How gladly, gladly I had died
(And life was very sweet that tide)
To save you from the least, light ill ?
How gladly I had borne your pain.

With one great pulse we seem'd to thrill,—
Nay, but we thrill'd with pulses twain.
Even if one had told me this,
"A poison lurks within your kiss,
Gall that shall turn to night his day :"

Thereon I straight had turned away—
Ay, tho' my heart had crack'd with pain—
And never kiss'd your lips again.
At night, or when the daylight nears,
I hear the other women weep ;
My own heart's anguish lies too deep
For the soft rain and pain of tears.
I think my heart has turn'd to stone,
A dull, dead weight that hurts my breast ;
Here, on my pallet-bed alone,
I keep apart from all the rest.
Wide-eyed I lie upon my bed,
I often cannot sleep all night ;
The future and the past are dead,
There is no thought can bring delight.
All night I lie and think and think ;
If my heart were not made of stone,
But flesh and blood, it needs must shrink
Before such thoughts. Was ever known
A woman with a heart of stone ?
The doctor says that I shall die.
It may be so, yet what care I ?
Endless reposing from the strife ?
Death do I trust no more than life.

For one thing is like one arrayed,
And there is neither false nor true ;
But in a hideous masquerade
All things dance on, the ages through.
And good is evil, evil good ;
Nothing is known or understood
Save only Pain. I have no faith
In God or Devil, Life or Death.
The doctor says that I shall die.
You, that I knew in days gone by,
I fain would see your face once more,
Con well its features o'er and o'er ;

And touch your hand and feel your kiss,
Look in your eyes and tell you this :
That all is done, that I am free ;
That you, through all eternity,
Have neither part nor lot in me.

Christopher Found.

I.

AT last ; so this is you, my dear !
How should I guess to find you here ?
So long, so long, I sought in vain
In many cities, many lands,
With straining eyes and groping hands ;
The people marvelled at my pain.
They said : "But sure, the woman's mad ;
What ails her, we should like to know,
That she should be so wan and sad,
And silent through the revels go ?"
They clacked with such a sorry stir !
Was I to tell ? were they to know
That I had lost you, Christopher ?
Will you forgive me for one thing ?
Whiles, when a stranger came my way,
My heart would beat and I would say :
" Here's Christopher !" —then lingering
With longer gaze, would turn away

Cold, sick at heart. My dear, I know
You will forgive me for this thing.
It is so very long ago
Since I have seen your face—till now ;
Now that I see it—lip and brow,
Eyes, nostril, chin, alive and clear ;
Last time was long ago ; I know
This thing you will forgive me, dear.

II.

There is no Heaven—This is the best ;
O hold me closer to your breast ;
Let your face lean upon my face,
That there no longer shall be space
Between our lips, between our eyes.
I feel your bosom's fall and rise.
O hold me near and yet more near ;
Ah sweet ; I wonder do you know

How lone and cold, how sad and drear,
Was I a little while ago ;
Sick of the stress, the strife, the stir ;
But I have found you, Christopher.

    III.

If only you had come before !
(This is the thing I most deplore)

A seemlier woman you had found,
More calm, by courtesies more bound,
Less quick to greet you, more subdued
Of appetite ; of slower mood.
But ah ! you come so late, so late !
This time of day I can't pretend
With slight, sweet things to satiate
The hunger-cravings. Nay, my friend,
I cannot blush and turn and tremble,
Wax loth as younger maidens do.
Ah, Christopher, with you, with you,
You would not wish me to dissemble ?

    IV.

So long have all the days been meagre,
With empty platter, empty cup,
No meats nor sweets to do me pleasure,
That if I crave—is it over-eager,
The deepest draught, the fullest measure,
The beaker to the brim poured up ?

    V.

Shelley, that sprite from the spheres above,
Says, and would make the matter clear,
That love divided is larger love ;—
We'll leave those things to the bards, my dear.

For you never wrote a verse, you see ;
And I—my verse is not fair nor new.
Till the world be dead, you shall love but me,
Till the stars have ceased, I shall love but you.

EPILOGUE.

Thus ran the words; or rather, thus did run
Their purport. Idly seeking in the chest
(You see it yonder), I had found them there:
Some blotted sheets of paper in a case,
With a woman's name writ on it: "Adelaide."
Twice on the writing there was scored the date
Of ten years back; and where the words had end
Was left a space, a dash, a half-writ word,
As tho' the writer minded, presently
The matter to pursue.
   I questioned her,
That worthy, worthy soul, my châtelaine,
Who, nothing loth, made answer.
     There had been
Another lodger ere I had the rooms,
Three months gone by—a woman.
      "Young, sir? No.
Must have seen forty if she'd seen a day!
A lonesome woman; hadn't many friends;
Wrote books, I think, and things for newspapers.

Short in her temper—eyes would flash and flame
At times, till I was frightened. Paid her rent
Most regular, like a lady.
    Ten years back,
They say (at least Ann Brown says), ten years back
The lady had a lover. Even then
She must have been no chicken.
     Three months since
She died. Well, well, the Lord is kind and just.
I did my best to tend her, yet indeed
It's bad for trade to have a lodger die.
Her brother came, a week before she died:
Buried her, took her things, threw in the fire
The littered heaps of paper.
     Yes, the sheets,
They must have been forgotten in the chest;—
I never knew her name was Adelaide."

A Dirge.

"Mein Herz, mein Herz ist traurig
doch lustig leuchtet der Mai"

THERE'S May amid the meadows,
   There's May amid the trees ;
Her May-time note the cuckoo
   Sends forth upon the breeze.

Above the rippling river
   May swallows skim and dart ;
November and December
   Keep watch within my heart.

The spring breathes in the breezes,
   The woods with wood-notes ring,
And all the budding hedgerows
   Are fragrant of the spring.

In secret, silent places
   The live green things upstart ;
Ice-bound, ice-crown'd dwells winter
   For ever in my heart.

Upon the bridge I linger,
   Near where the lime-trees grow ;
Above, swart birds are circling,
   Beneath, the stream runs slow.

A stripling and a maiden
   Come wand'ring up the way ;
His eyes are glad with springtime,
   Her face is fair with May.

Of warmth the sun and sweetness
   All nature takes a part ;
The ice of all the ages
   Weighs down upon my heart.

The Sick Man and the Nightingale.

(From Lenau.)

SO late, and yet a nightingale ?
Long since have dropp'd the blossoms pale,
The summer fields are ripening,
   And yet a sound of spring ?

O tell me, didst thou come to hear,
Sweet Spring, that I should die this year ;
And call'st across from the far shore
   To me one greeting more ?

To Death.

(From Lenau.)

IF within my heart there's mould,
If the flame of Poesy
And the flame of Love grow cold,
Slay my body utterly.

Swiftly, pause not nor delay ;
Let not my life's field be spread
With the ash of feelings dead,
Let thy singer soar away.

A June-Tide Echo.

(After a Richter Concert.)

IN the long, sad time, when the sky was grey,
   And the keen blast blew through the city drear,
When delight had fled from the night and the day,
   My chill heart whispered, " June will be here !

" June with its roses a-sway in the sun,
   Its glory of green on mead and tree."
Lo, now the sweet June-tide is nearly done,
   June-tide, and never a joy for me

Is it so much of the gods that I pray ?
   Sure craved man never so slight a boon !
To be glad and glad in my heart one day—
   One perfect day of the perfect June.

Sweet sounds to-night rose up, wave upon wave ;
   Sweet dreams were afloat in the balmy air.
This is the boon of the gods that I crave—
   To be glad, as the music and night were fair.

For once, for one fleeting hour, to hold
   The fair shape the music that rose and fell
Revealed and concealed like a veiling fold ;
   To catch for an instant the sweet June spell.

For once, for one hour, to catch and keep
   The sweet June secret that mocks my heart ;
Now lurking calm, like a thing asleep,
   Now hither and thither with start and dart.

Then the sick, slow grief of the weary years,
   The slow, sick grief and the sudden pain ;
The long days of labour, the nights of tears—
   No more these things would I hold in vain.

I would hold my life as a thing of worth ;
   Pour praise to the gods for a precious thing.
Lo, June in her fairness is on earth,
   And never a joy does the niggard bring.

To Lallie.

(Outside the British Museum.)
UP those Museum steps you came,
And straightway all my blood was flame,
 O Lallie, Lallie !

The world (I had been feeling low)
In one short moment's space did grow
 A happy valley.

There was a friend, my friend, with you ;
A meagre dame, in peacock blue
 Apparelled quaintly ;

This poet-heart went pit-a-pat ;
I bowed and smiled and raised my hat ;
 You nodded—faintly.

My heart was full as full could be;
You had not got a word for me,
 Not one short greeting ;

That nonchalant small nod you gave
(The tyrant's motion to the slave)
 Sole mark'd our meeting.

Is it so long ? Do you forget
That first and last time that we met ?
 The time was summer ;

The trees were green ; the sky was blue ;
Our host presented me to you—
 A tardy comer.

You look'd demure, but when you spoke
You made a little, funny joke,
 Yet half pathetic.

Your gown was grey, I recollect,
I think you patronized the sect
 They call "æsthetic."

I brought you strawberries and cream,
I plied you long about a stream
    With duckweed laden ;

We solemnly discussed the—heat.
I found you shy and very sweet,
    A rosebud maiden.

Ah me, to-day ! You passed inside
To where the marble gods abide :
    Hermes, Apollo,

Sweet Aphrodite, Pan ; and where,
For aye reclined, a headless fair
    Beats all fairs hollow.

And I, I went upon my way,
Well—rather sadder, let us say ;
    The world looked flatter.

I had been sad enough before,
A little less, a little more,
    What does it matter ?

In a Minor Key.

(AN ECHO FROM A LARGER LYRE.)

THAT was love that I had before
   Years ago, when my heart was young ;
Ev'ry smile was a gem you wore ;
   Ev'ry word was a sweet song sung.

You came—all my pulses burn'd and beat.
   (O sweet wild throbs of an early day !)
You went—with the last dear sound of your feet
   The light wax'd dim and the place grew grey.

And I us'd to pace with a stealthy tread
   By a certain house which is under a hill ;
A cottage stands near, wall'd white, roof'd red—
   Tall trees grow thick—I can see it still !

How I us'd to watch with a hope that was fear
   For the least swift glimpse of your gown's dear fold !
(You wore blue gowns in those days, my dear—
   One light for summer, one dark for cold.)

Tears and verses I shed for you in show'rs ;
   I would have staked my soul for a kiss ;
Tribute daily I brought you of flow'rs,
   Rose, lily, your favourite eucharis.

There came a day we were doomed to part ;
   There's a queer, small gate at the foot of a slope :
We parted there—and I thought my heart
   Had parted for ever from love and hope.

         * * * * *

Is it love that I have to-day ?
   Love, that bloom'd early, has it bloom'd late
For me, that, clothed in my spirit's grey,
   Sit in the stillness and stare at Fate ?

Song nor sonnet for you I've penned,
   Nor passionate paced by your home's wide wall

I have brought you never a flow'r, my friend,
   Never a tear for your sake let fall.

And yet—and yet—ah, who understands ?
   We men and women are complex things !
A hundred tunes Fate's inexorable hands
   May play on the sensitive soul-strings.

Webs of strange patterns we weave (each owns)
   From colour and sound; and like unto these,
Soul has its tones and its semitones,
   Mind has its major and minor keys.

Your face (men pass it without a word)
   It haunts my dreams like an odd, sweet strain ;
When your name is spoken my soul is stirr'd
   In its deepest depths with a dull, dim pain.

I paced, in the damp grey mist, last night
   In the streets (an hour) to see you pass :
Yet I do not think that I love you—quite ;
   What's felt so finely 'twere coarse to class.

And yet—and yet—I scarce can tell why
   (As I said, we are riddles and hard to read),
If the world went ill with you, and I
   Could help with a hidden hand your need ;

But, ere I could reach you where you lay,
   Must strength and substance and honour spend ;
Journey long journeys by night and day—
   Somehow, I think I should come, my friend !

A Farewell.

(After Heine.)

THE sad rain falls from Heaven,
   A sad bird pipes and sings ;
I am sitting here at my window
   And watching the spires of "King's."

O fairest of all fair places,
   Sweetest of all sweet towns !
With the birds, and the greyness and greenness,
   And the men in caps and gowns.

All they that dwell within thee,
   To leave are ever loth,
For one man gets friends, and another
   Gets honour, and one gets both.

The sad rain falls from Heaven ;
   My heart is great with woe—
I have neither a friend nor honour,
   Yet I am sorry to go.

A Cross-Road Epitaph.

"Am Kreuzweg wird begraben
Wer selber brachte sich um."

WHEN first the world grew dark to me
I call'd on God, yet came not he.
Whereon, as wearier wax'd my lot,
On Love I call'd, but Love came not.
When a worse evil did befall,
Death, on thee only did I call.

Epitaph.

(On a Commonplace Person Who Died in Bed.)

THIS is the end of him, here he lies :
The dust in his throat, the worm in his eyes,
The mould in his mouth, the turf on his breast ;
This is the end of him, this is best.
He will never lie on his couch awake,
Wide-eyed, tearless, till dim daybreak.
Never again will he smile and smile
When his heart is breaking all the while.
He will never stretch out his hands in vain
Groping and groping—never again.
Never ask for bread, get a stone instead,
Never pretend that the stone is bread.
Never sway and sway 'twixt the false and true,
Weighing and noting the long hours through.
Never ache and ache with the chok'd-up sighs ;
This is the end of him, here he lies.

Sonnet.

MOST wonderful and strange it seems, that I
Who but a little time ago was tost
High on the waves of passion and of pain,
With aching heart and wildly throbbing brain,
Who peered into the darkness, deeming vain
All things there found if but One thing were lost,
Thus calm and still and silent here should lie,
Watching and waiting,—waiting passively.
The dark has faded, and before mine eyes
Have long, grey flats expanded, dim and bare ;
And through the changing guises all things wear
Inevitable Law I recognise :
Yet in my heart a hint of feeling lies
Which half a hope and half is a despair.

Translated from Geibel.

O SAY, thou wild, thou oft-deceived heart,
What mean these noisy throbbings in my breast?
After thy long, unutterable woe
    Wouldst thou not rest?

Fall'n from Life's tree the sweet rose-blossom lies,
And fragrant youth has fled. What made to seem
This earth as fair to thee as Paradise,
    Was all a dream.

The blossom fell, the thorn was left to me;
Deep from the wound the blood-drops ever flow,
All that I have are yearnings, wild desires,
    And wrath and woe.

They brought me Lethe's water, saying, "Drink!"
"Drink, for the draught is sweet," I heard them say,
"Shalt learn how soft a thing forgetting is."
    I answered: "Nay."

What tho' indeed it were an idle cheat,
Nathless to me 'twas very fair and blest:
With every breath I draw I know that love
    Reigns in my breast.

Let me go forth,—and thou, my heart, bleed on:
A lonely spot I seek by night and day,
That love and sorrow I may there breathe forth
    In a last lay.

CPSIA information can be obtained at www.ICGtesting.com
Printed in the USA
BVOW02s0106211113

336837BV00003B/960/P